THE SOUTH HAMS
Photographs by Bob Croxford

The South Hams is a fascinating corner of Devon. Totnes with its bridge across the street acts as a gateway to this land of green fields, narrow lanes, sailing centres, estuaries and beaches. Dartmouth with its boat filled estuary is guarded by a 15C Castle. Salcombe has a reputation for sailing. Sandy coves at Blackpool Sands, East Portlemouth, Bantham, Burgh Island, Wonwell and other places are ideal for relaxing on the beach.

Published by Atmosphere
Willis Vean
Mullion Cornwall TR12 7DF
England
Tel 01326 240 180
email info@atmosphere.co.uk

Cover : Blackpool Sands

ISBN 9521850 9 1

Printed and bound in Italy

Frontispiece : Postbox at Penquit

Sailing at Salcombe

Totnes

Stoke Gabriel
　　　　　　　　　Waddeton

Dittisham

Dartmouth

Dartmouth Castle

View towards Kingswear from Dartmouth

Bayard's Cove, Dartmouth

Kingswear from Dartmouth   *The Royal Naval College Dartmouth*

Blackpool Sands   *Slapton*

Hallsands

WW2 Memorial at Slapton

Start Point

Hallsands Beach

Start Point Lighthouse

Western Cove   *Prawle Point*

Kingsbridge Estuary from East Portlemouth

Southpool Creek

East Portlemouth from Salcombe

Salcombe

Salcombe

Kingsbridge Estuary

Salcombe

Hope Cove

Hope Cove

Thurlestone Beach

Hope Cove

Kingsbridge

Lane nr Kingsbridge

South Pool

Bantham Boat House

Burgh Island Sunset

Burgh Island

Wonwell Beach

Newton Ferrers   *Noss Mayo*

Wembury

Mouthstone Point

*View over farmland towards Dartmoor with
Modbury in the distance*

River Avon

Ivybridge and the River Erme

Modbury

Ashburton

Buckfast Abbey

The Dart Valley Line and the River Dart   *Overleaf : Tree near Dartmouth*